T0150979

# THE LITTLE BOOK OF
# PROSECCO

Published by OH!
20 Mortimer Street
London W1T 3JW

**Disclaimer:**

ISBN 978-1-80069-019-6

Compiled by: Theresa Bebbington
Editorial: Lisa Dyer
Project manager: Russell Porter
Design: Tony Seddon
Production: Freencky Portas

A CIP catalogue record for this book is available from the British Library

Printed in China

10 9 8 7 6 5 4 3 2

Images: freepik.com

# THE LITTLE BOOK OF
# PROSECCO

## SPARKLING PERFECTION

# CONTENTS

# *Save Water: Drink Prosecco*

Who doesn't love a chilled glass of Prosecco? Champagne's lighter, more affordable Italian cousin is a refreshing, dry sparkling wine, perfect for every occasion. From a summer tipple to a tasty cocktail or a festive fizz, you just can't beat it. And as global sales would indicate, Prosecco is the new black. *The Little Book of Prosecco* celebrates our love affair with this Italian bubbly.

In the first chapter "In Vino Veritas", you'll discover Prosecco's long history – how it was once considered an elixir to long life, how it wasn't always a sparkling wine and how the Father of Prosecco transformed it into the not-so-sweet Prosecco we love today. "Prosecco Superiore" follows with a look at how Prosecco is produced, from the grapes on the vines to the sparkling wine in the bottle – and why true Prosecco comes from only nine provinces in Italy. You'll learn the difference between spumante and frizzante, and between DOC and DOCG. For a lighter mood, the "Sparkling Froth" chapter is filled with Prosecco-related anecdotes and trivia, from vine thieves to celebrity producers to Prosecco-filled ATM machines.

"Tasting Notes" focuses on the art of drinking Prosecco, from how to choose a good bottle to how to keep an opened bottle bubbly. While Prosecco is perfect in a chilled glass on its own, why not treat yourself to a cocktail featuring this fizz? Having friends around? Prosecco is perfect for a punch. Turn to "Cocktails & Punches" for a generous concoction of recipes. To round off your experience, sit back with your feet up and a glass of Prosecco in hand, and turn to "Popping Out" to enjoy quirky quotes and proverbs to pair with your glass of fizz.

Bubbling with Prosecco-infused wit and wisdom, and mixed with recipes for some of Italy's most iconic Prosecco cocktails, *The Little Book of Prosecco* is a sparkling celebration of one of the world's best-loved wines – it will have you reaching for a bottle and popping that cork (safely, of course) in no time.

CHAPTER
**ONE**

"In wine there is truth" – the history behind Prosecco.

# The First Sip of Wine

An ancient Persian fable tells of a princess who lost favour with the king and tried to poison herself with spoilt grapes, but instead she became intoxicated. She continued to enjoy the fermented grapes, and her improved demeanour restored her to the king's favour. And that is the start of our love affair with wine.

# Empress's Elixir for Long Life

The wife of Emperor Octavian Augustus, Empress Livia (58 BC–AD 29) reached a respectful age in good health, which she contributed to drinking the "Pucino" wine loved by Romans – it came from the Prosecco area. There is an account of this story in *Natural History* by Pliny the Elder (AD 23–79).

**"**

*Here growes the wine Pucinum, now called Prosecho, much celebrated by Pliny.*

**"**

**Fynes Morson (1593)**

*Found in the travel notes of an English gentleman, the text provides a connection between Pucino and Prosecco. The notes indicate that the wine was already popular at the time.*

# Proseco, the Town

The small town in the Trieste province in north-eastern Italy known as "Prosech", "Prosecum" or modern "Proseco" was first mentioned in the mid-thirteenth century in a deed for the rental of four vineyards.

**"**

*...and now I would like so much
to wet my mouth with the
Prosecco from Monteberico,
enjoying its apple bouquet.
It's the perfect Prosecco, a true
example for all others.*

**"**

**From a poem by Aureliano Acanti,
published in *Il Roccolo Ditirambo* in Venice in 1754.**

# Tuscan Essay

In the 1773 essay "Oenologia Toscana" by Villafranchi, the author noted that the wine called "Prosecco" was made with grapes that came from "the slope of Contuel Mountain facing the Adriatic Sea, a few miles away from Tieste".

The town of Prosecco is about 10km (6 miles) from Trieste.

# Glera's Origins

Prosecco is made mostly with the Glera grape (*see page 38*), but its history is shrouded in mystery.

It is believed that the grape first appeared along the Dalmatian coast or in Slovenia. However, the grape's cultivation had reached the Veneto and Friuli hills by the eighteenth century and spread from there.

# Premium Cartizze

One of the best Proseccos is considered to be Cartizze, but theories differ on the origins of this name.

It could come from *gardizze*, the term people from Valdobbiadene use for the grapes' drying racks. Or it could come from the *cardo* (thistle) flower.

# Modern Times

Documents, such as one by Francesco Maria Malvolti, begin to mention the Prosecco grape from the beginning of the nineteenth century. This is considered the beginning of Prosecco's modern history, when it was clear Prosecco referred to the white wine.

# Setting Up School

Antonio Carpenè Sr is considered
the Father of Prosecco. Not only
was he a chemist who refined
the winemaking process and
championed industry standards,
he established the Istituto Cerletti
in Conegliano in 1876 – Italy's first
school of viticulture and enology.
It continues to be the region's top
winemaking institution today.

# A New Bubbly Invention

In 1895 Federico Martinotti, a winemaker in Asti, invented the Martinotti method for trapping bubbles in wine fermented in large steel tanks.

By using this tank method, producers could make sparkling wine in large volumes and therefore at a lower cost.

# One Method, Many Names

The Martinotti method is also known as the Charmat method, after Eugène Charmat, a Frenchman who made improvements on Martinotti's invention in 1907.

Other terms for this method include the tank method, *metodo Italiano* and *cuve close*, meaning "sealed tank" (from the French *cuvée*, meaning "vat").

# Flat Origins

The original Prosecco drunk before the invention of the Martinotti (Charmat) tank method would have been flat.

# From Sweet to Dry

Prosecco sipped before the 1960s would have been on the sweeter end of the spectrum.

With improved production methods and viticulture, the Prosecco we drink today has moved towards a drier, more elegant style.

# Timeline of the Twentieth Century Dates

**1962:** The Consortium for the Protection of Prosecco in Conegliano and Valdobbiadene was established by 11 producers.

**1966:** Winding through Conegliano and Valdobbiadene, the 120km (75-mile) Prosecco Route was established, the first wine route in Italy.

**1969:** Controlled Designation of Origin, or DOC, was given to Prosecco produced by 15 municipalities in Conegliano and Valdobbiadene.

**1973:** DOC recognition was also established for Asolo and Montello.

**2003:** The 15 municipalities of the Prosecco DOC were awarded Prime Italian Sparkling Wine District status.

# Protecting Prosecco Vineyards

The Italian government made an all-encompassing upgrade of nine provinces from IGT (*Indicazione Geografica Tipica*) to DOC (*Denominazione di Origine Controllata*) in 2009.

Bottles with the Prosecco DOC label are produced in only these regions and their production elsewhere is prohibited.

# Recognizing the Best

The Italian government also upgraded the Conegliano-Valdobbiadene Prosecco DOC zones to DOCG (*Denominazione di Origine Controllata e Garantita*) status in 2009. Among the new regulations that come with this status, yields were reduced in these zones to help improve quality.

# Grape Name

Before receiving DOC status, Prosecco was the term used for both the grape and the region.

With DOC protection, the grape is now officially identified by its viniferous name: Glera. If a wine is produced in the region but not within the DOC regulations, it must be labelled Glera IGT and cannot be called Prosecco.

# Outselling Champagne

For the first time, between 2013 and 2014, Prosecco outsold Champagne.

As well as being popular in Italy, Prosecco had strong sells in the United Kingdom, Germany and the United States – and the nation with the largest increase in sales was France!

# Seal of Approval

The Prosecco DOC Consortium not only works with industry professionals to support winegrowers in improving their production, it is responsible for promoting and protecting Prosecco's reputation.

If a bottle has its official secure seal, it's a guarantee that the bottle was produced in compliance with Prosecco DOC regulations and in the approved provinces.

As well as a seal, the label will include:

- **Prosecco DOC**
(Registered Designation of Origin)

- *Prodotto in Italia*
(Made in Italy)

- *Fascetta di Stato*
(State mark and seal)

- **Spumante or Frizzante designation**

# World Heritage Status

The hills and landscape of Conegliano and Valdobbiadene are considered so unique and beautiful that they earned a place on the UNESCO World Heritage List in July 2019.

The territory given this honour is only 97sq km (37½ square miles) of vines.

# Towards Environmental Sustainability

The Wine Protocol is a set of rules with the purpose of changing agriculture over time to participate in less-invasive and damaging practices.

The Producers' Consortium for Prosecco Superiore DOCG has followed this set of rules since 2011.

**"**

*A glass of wine can make a friend; a barrel can make a friendship."*

**"**

**Unknown**

# New Partners

As of 2016, the Producers' Consortium for Prosecco Superiore DOCG in Italy has partnered with the Cité des Civilizations du Vin in Bordeaux, a famous French cultural institution dedicated to international wine.

Who would have thought such a liaison would develop in what would seem to be competing countries?

CHAPTER
**TWO**

# Prosecco Superiore

From vine to bottle,
all there is to know about
producing Prosecco.

# The Special Prosecco Grape

Prosecco is made from the Italian grape called Glera, which is native to and has grown in north-eastern Italy since ancient Roman times. Glera may be a "white" grape, but the vine produces golden-yellow grapes growing on dark brown branches. Glera has a high acidity and light body suitable for sparkling wine.

# Additional Grapes

Although Glera is the primary variety for making Prosecco, up to 15 per cent of other varieties can be combined with it.

These include Bianchetta Trevigiana, Chardonnay, Glera Iunga, Perera, Pinot Bianco, Pinot Grigio, Pino Nero and Verdiso grapes.

# Just the Right Weather

The Prosecco region is nestled between the Dolomite Mountains and Adriatic Sea. It has warm, sunny days and cool evenings influenced by its location, and an average annual rainfall of 152cm (60 inches).

The long days and diurnal temperature shift (the difference between day and night temperatures) are exactly right for producing the Glera grapes.

# The Perfect Soils

Over the centuries, the original alluvial soils have evolved, and today's clay-loam soils are rich in minerals and micro-elements, perfect for growing Glera grapes.

The hilly regions have calcium-rich marl and flysch sandstone soils, but in the plains and valleys, the soils are clay, sand and gravel.

# Terraces

In some areas, such as Conegliano Valdobbiadene, the slopes on the hills are particularly steep, making the soils difficult to cultivate.

The solution? Create terracing! Over the years, the locals created *ciglione* terracing, using grassy ground instead of stonewalls to retain the soil.

# There's Trouble in Them There Hills

An analysis of the vineyards between Valdobbiadene and Conegliano indicates that 400,000 tonnes of soil is lost each year.

For each bottle of Prosecco produced, 4.4kg (9¾ pounds) of soil is lost.

# Heard it on the Grapevine

To grow the healthiest, most productive vines, grapevines are vertically trained on trellises.

To keep the yields in check and encourage the development of the remaining grapes, green grapes are harvested, and the vines are pinched and tied in place.

**66**

*And that you may the less marvel at my words, Look at the sun's heat that becomes wine when combine with the juice that flows from the vine.*

**99**

**Dante Alighieri (1265–1321)**

# Harvest Time

The sugars, acidity and aromatics of the grapes reach their peak in the first weeks of September, so this is when grapes are harvested.

The grapes need to be crushed and have their stems removed before being fermented.

# Prosecco Millesimato

This is the term given to Prosecco when at least 85 per cent of its grapes are harvested in the same year.

If you find *millesimato* on a label, you should expect it to be a particularly good bottle of bubbly.

# Double Bubble

To create the bubbles, a sparkling wine goes through two fermentation processes.

The first fermentation creates the base wine; in the second one, yeast converts sugar into alcohol and carbon dioxide. Being in a sealed environment, the carbon dioxide forms bubbles.

# Tanked

Prosecco uses the Charmat, or Martinotti, tank method for the second fermentation stage, which takes place in a large pressurized steel tank. It creates larger bubbles than the traditional (classic) method used for Champagne, where the second fermentation takes place in bottles.

# A Primer on Bubbles

Although Prosecco is best known as a sparkling wine with bubbles, it can also be produced with little or no bubbles.

There are different terms for the amount of bubbliness and sugar content.

# Tranquillo
*("quiet")*:

flat, with no bubbles; straw yellow in colour; fruity and floral aromas of apple, pear, almond and acacia flowers; 10.5% volume minimum alcohol content. Serve at 8–10°C (46–50°F).

# Frizzante
*("lightly sparking")*:

with light, less persistent bubbles; varying intensities of straw yellow; fruity and floral aromas of apple, pear, pear and wisteria; 9% volume minimum alcohol content. Serve at 8–10°C (46–50°F).

# Spumante

*("sparkling"):*

persistent bubbles; varying intensities of straw yellow in colour; aromas of apple, rose and banana; 11% volume minimum alcohol content.

Spumante is further categorized by residual sugar content:

# Brut

*(6–12 g/l):*

hints of citrus aromas with vegetal notes.
Serve at 6–8°C (43–47°F).

# Extra Dry

*(12–17 g/l):*

fruity and floral aromas with apple, pear
and citrus. Serve at 6–8°C (43–47°F).

# Dry

*(12–32 g/l):*

fruity aromas of apple and peach. Serve
at 6°C (43°F).

# Applying Pressure

Ever wonder why some Prosecco is bubblier than others?

It is down to how much atmospheres of pressure (ATM) is inside the bottle:

*Spumante:* 1-3 atm

*Frizzante:* 1–1.5 atm

*Tranquillo:* less than 1 atm

# Getting Corked

A sparkling wine cork starts out as a cylindrical shape, but to withstand the pressure inside, a few cork discs are glued on to the main cork body.

When the cork is removed, the discs expand more rapidly than the main body, creating the classic mushroom-shaped sparkling wine cork.

# 8 Steps to Making Prosecco

**1.** Harvest the grapes.

**2.** Press the grapes to obtain the "must", a dense liquid substance.

**3.** Rest the must in tanks, decanting the heaviest parts.

**4.** Place the clear decanted must into steel cylinders at a controlled temperature.

**5.** Add yeast to start fermentation so the must becomes a "base wine".

**6.** Enrich the base wine with other batches to create specific characteristics, creating the "cuvée".

**7.** Decant the wine into a large pressure chamber for a second fermentation, or refermentation, with added yeasts and sugar.

**8.** After 30 to 90 days, the sparkling wine is ready for bottling – but it can't be sold for another 40 days.

# Setting Prosecco Apart from Champagne

*Location:* Prosecco can be made only in a designated area in Italy and Champagne in a designated area of France.

*Grapes:* Prosecco is produced from the Glera variety; Champagne uses Chardonnay, Pinot Noir and Pinot Meunier.

*Fermenting method:* Prosecco is fermented in steel tanks, Champagne in bottles.

*Carbonation:* The pressure applied is different; Prosecco has a softer carbonation than Champagne.

*Flavour:* Prosecco has fresh fruit notes, Champagne a nuttier, toasty character.

*Cost:* Champagne is more expensive due to its elaborate production method. It must mature for at least 15 months, whereas Prosecco is ready within weeks of bottling.

*Consumption:* Prosecco is best for making cocktails or punches, Champagne for special occasions.

# Guide to Italy's Tier of Wine Classification

## DOCG

*(Denominazione di Origine Controllata e Garantita):*

The top of the tier, a wine in this classification has been produced by controlled production methods and its quality is guaranteed.

Strict rules limit the choice of grape varieties, ripeness and yields, winemaking techniques and ageing time.

# DOC

*(Denominazione di Origine Controllata):*

This middle tier includes almost all traditional Italian wine styles, which must be produced following laws governing the production area, grape varieties and wine style.

The wines must be produced and bottled in the specified DOC zone.

# ITG
*(Indicazione Geografica Tipica):*

The region of origin is the main focus of this wine category. It can include high-quality wines that fail to obtain DOC or DOCG status due to using grape varieties not allowed in these classifications.

## *Vino da Tavola:*
This is Italian for "table wine" and represents the most basic of Italian wines.

**❝**

*This wine is too good for toast-drinking my dear. You don't want to mix emotions up with a wine like that.*

**❞**

Count Mippipopolous in *The Sun Also Rises*,
by Ernest Hemingway (1926)

# Prosecco DOC

Prosecco is produced in the unique environmental conditions found in the Prosecco DOC zone in north-eastern Italy.

There are only nine provinces in the zone: four provinces are in Friuli-Venezia-Giulia (*Gorizia, Pordenone, Trieste* and *Udine*), and five provinces are in Veneto (*Belluno, Padua, Treviso, Venice* and *Vicenza*).

## *Where There Are Rules, There Are Also Exceptions*

Although forming part of the Prosecco DOC area, Treviso and Trieste are historically important Prosecco provinces.
This has been acknowledged by the Italian government, which allows the two areas to label their bottles respectively "Prosecco DOC Treviso" and "Prosecco DOC Trieste".

# Prosecco DOC in Numbers

The Prosecco DOC zone covers 23,000 hectares (56,835 acres).

The vineyards are allowed a maximum yield of 180,000kg (396,800lbs) of fruit per hectare.

There are 11,102 vineyards in the zone.

The zone has 1,211 wineries.

There are 348 winemakers in the area.

The average annual DOC production yields 464 million bottles of Prosecco.

Sparkling wine comprises 83 per cent of the region's production.

Semi-sparkling wine comprises 17 per cent of the region's production.

Still wine comprises one per cent of the region's production.

# Prosecco DOCG

Only two zones have been awarded the more stringent DOCG label for the excellent quality of their Prosecco: the hills of Asolo and Conegliano-Valdobbiadene, which are both located in the province of Treviso.

# Four to One

About 80 per cent of all Prosecco drunk in Italy and worldwide comes from one territory: Veneto. The remaining 20 per cent is produced in Friuli-Venezia-Giulia.

# Piemonte Prosecco?

How can Prosecco come from Piemonte (Piedmont) if it's not in the DOC zone? Well, there are some special exceptions, such as when "the production of the wine is part of a well-consolidated tradition". This applies to Piemonte – but the grapes must still come from a DOC or DOCG region.

# Make Mine Rosé

In May 2020, the Producers' Consortium for Prosecco DOC decided to allow the production of a rosé Prosecco. As well as the minimum of 85 per cent Glera grapes, winemakers can add 10–15 per cent Pinot Nero (aka Pinot Noir) to obtain a "brilliant, more or less intense rose hue".

# Fermented Prosecco

A traditional, more natural way to produce Prosecco involves complete fermentation in the bottle with the lees (sediment).

The result is *col fondo*, a cloudier, less fizzy and drier version of Prosecco. Most Prosecco was produced this way until steel vats were introduced in the 1970s.

**"**

*...then the streams would run with wine instead of water and the whole forest would give up to jollification for weeks on end.*

**"**

C. S. Lewis, *The Lion, the Witch and the Wardrobe* (1950)

# Best of the Best

The hills of Asolo and the Conegliano-Valdobbiadene provide the exact microclimate and soils needed for growing Glera grapes and producing the best Prosecco.

However, two particular selections of the same wine are noted for being of premium quality:

# Rive:

If you find "Rive" on a wine label, the grapes have come from the steepest, most inaccessible slopes of Conegliano-Valdobbiadene. Rive is used only for making sparkling wine.

# Cartizze:

A small area of only about 100 hectares (250 acres) near Valdobbiadene produces grapes for Prosecco Superiore di Cartizze. Found on the steepest slopes of the Santo Stefano, Saccol and San Pietro di Barbozza hills, the soils were once part of a seabed, giving it special qualities.

CHAPTER
**THREE**

# Tasting Notes

Fizzy facts on
enjoying Prosecco.

# What Does Prosecco Taste Like?

Prosecco's aromas and flavours have been described as being reminiscent of:

Bananas
Green apples
Green fruits
Lemon zest
Lime zest
Melon
Peach
Pears

Pineapples
Red apples
Tropical fruits
White blossoms/
flowers
Yellow blossoms/
flowers

**"**

*Friends don't let friends drink Prosecco alone.*

**"**

**Unknown**

# Choosing a Good Bottle of Bubbly

Prosecco doesn't have the same protected status provided for Champagne, so here are a few tips for choosing a bottle.

***Look for an Italian product:*** check the label to make sure it's produced in Italy – not all bottles are.

### *Ensure it's made from the Glera grape:*

look for DOC or DOCG on the label – these initials guarantee that they were used (*see pages 60-1*). If you do find "Glera" on the label, it means it can be an inferior bottle not up to scratch to earn one of these labels.

### *Want the best?*

Choose DOCG rather DOC, and look for Rive or – for the best of them all – Catizze.

# Dry or Sweet – Your Choice

"Extra Brut" is the Prosecco to choose if you prefer a very dry tipple; "Brut" is slightly sweeter. However, "Extra Dry", despite it's name, is actually sweeter than the two bruts, and "Dry" is the sweetest of them all.

And there's a new entry: "Ultra Brut" has no sugar in it, so expect it to be particularly dry.

# Bottle with Bling

Casanova Prosecco limited "Swarovski Edition" DOC comes in bottles covered in Swarovski crystals (and certificates of authenticity). As of 2021, their 750ml bottle, with 3,370 crystals, has a price tag of about £1,365 ($1,820).

For their 1.5L magnum bottle, covered with 6,145 crystals: £2,400 ($3,200).

# How to Impress Your Friends When Choosing Prosecco

When the waiter presents the bubbly, check the neck of the bottle: if there's a blue label it's DOC; if it's brown, it's DOCG – go for brown.

Planning to splash out for a special occasion? Ask your waiter if they serve Cartizze – or if there's a wine list, it may be in the Champagne section.

If your friend points to a cheap bottle on the wine list, point out it will be bog standard (DOC) Prosecco.

Ask how long the bottle has been stored, and turn down any bottle over a year old.

# For a Limited Time Only...

Even an unopened bottle of Prosecco has a limited shelf life – the recommendation is that you pop the cork and drink this sparkling wine within a year of purchasing.

# Chilling Facts

Prosecco is best served chilled, but don't store it in the fridge for too long - after a few days the cork can dry out, leaving to a demise of those lovely bubbles.

Instead, store in a cool dry place - the bottle needs chilling in the fridge for only a few hours before drinking it.

# Steps to Safe Corking

Follow the instructions below to safely remove a cork from a Prosecco bottle - and to avoid losing the bubbly once it's open.

**1.** Always chill the bottle before removing the cork (the bubbles expand when warm).

**2.** Despite what racing car drivers do, do NOT shake the bottle!

**3.** After removing the foil and wire cage, place a tea towel over the cork before holding the cork firmly and slowly twisting the base of the bottle.

**4.** Allow the cork to be pushed out naturally, but press down on it if it starts to come out too quickly.

# Saving the Bubbles

Once a bottle of Prosecco is opened, the bubbles will begin to dissipate until your sparkling spumante is more reminiscent of a bottle of flat tranquillo. However, if you use a sparkling wine stopper, the fizz will last another night – and keep it chilled in the fridge.

# Spoon in the Bottle?

An old wives' tale claims that putting the handle of a silver spoon into the neck of the bottle will keep it fizzy. However, a Stanford University study has burst the bubble on this old hack – it found no significant difference between bottles with and without a silver spoon.

# Shapely Glass

To allow for the best flavours from your drink, use a tulip-shaped glass that more closely resembles a wine glass than the flute used for Champagne.

The shape allows the aromas to breathe, which enhances the taste – and you'll also get more bubbly in the glass!

# Perfectly Imperfect Glass

A top-quality Prosecco glass has a tiny, laser-etched ring inside the bottom of the glass: this is a "nucleation point" to help form bubbles. The rest of the glass should be smooth to help prevent too much of a "mousse cap", which can trap aromas and affect the taste.

# Clean Glasses, More Bubbles

Traces of washing-up liquid, or fabric softener if you polish your glasses, can mean fewer bubbles in your glass.

One expert advises using a dishwasher to clean the glasses and polishing them with a microfibre cloth (that's not been clean with a fabric softener).

# To Cube or Not to Cube

That's a question easy to answer: if drinking Prosecco on it's own, do NOT add ice cubes, which can destroy the flavour as well as the fizziness.

However, if using Prosecco in a cocktail or punch, it depends on the mix – follow thc recipe.

# International Tipple

In 2018, 464 million bottles of Prosecco DOC were sold (not including Prosecco DOCG), at an estimate of 2.4 billion Euros (£2 billion/$2.5 billion)... but who drank all that Prosecco?

Europe is the biggest market with 72 per cent, or about 250 million bottles, with 25 per cent of that purchased by the Italians.

North Americans purchased 21.9 per cent, or about 76 million bottles.

Russia came in third, at 3.8 per cent.

Australia and New Zealand combined purchased 1.6 per cent.

South America bought 0.6 per cent.

Africa is at the bottom, at 0.1 per cent.

# Brits Just Love the Italian Fizz ...

In 2019, 560 million bottles of Prosecco were imported to the UK, making it Italy's No. 1 market. From the previous five years, sales of Prosecco in the UK increased by 163 per cent. Surprisingly, more British men – at 56 per cent – purchase the Italian bubbly than women!

# ... As Do the French

The French nation has opened it's arms to Italy's Prosecco, so much so that statistics released in February 2020 reveal that Prosecco exports to France increased by 35 per cent, making it the fastest growing market for Prosecco DOC. The increase is thought to be due to demand from a younger generation.

# Food Pairings

*Having breakfast?*
Try Mimosa with eggs.

*Want an afternoon treat?*
Have a glass with something sweet.

*Thirst quencher with pre-dinner nibbles?*
Serve with nuts, olives or crostini.

*Want a match for a light meal?*
Sip with a light seafood dish or salad.

*Need a palate cleanser?*
Try after creamy pastas or spicy curries.

# Dieting?

Prosecco has about 90 calories per glass: that's less than a banana - or about 20 minutes of pilates! Counting carbs?

Check the label for how sweet or dry it is. Ultra Brut or Brut Zero (a new entry) has no sugar, or go for Extra Brut (*see page 82*).

# A Healthy Tipple?

Of course, you should always drink responsibly (drink no more than 14 units a week, or about 9 small glasses of Prosecco), but the following health claims have been made about drinking Prosecco:

Sparkling wine contains polyphenols, which can lower blood pressure and improve blood circulation.

Sparkling wine contains zinc, magnesium and potassium, which can boost mood.

Prosecco may help keep lung tissues healthy.

One or two glasses can heighten a woman's sexual desire; the wine's antioxidants can increase blood flow in the nether regions.

One or two glasses a week can help delay the onset of dementia and slow down memory loss.

CHAPTER
**FOUR**

# Sparkling Froth

Light and fruity
anecdotes and trivia.

A bottle of Prosecco has
11–12 per cent ABV.

Compared to, say, a bottle of
red at 14 per cent ABV, its lower
alcohol content might explain
why Prosecco is less likely to
give you a hangover – however,
that only works if you don't keep
drinking it.

# The Great Prosecco Shortage of 2016

Prosecco producers have not always been able to keep up with the increased worldwide demand for the fizzy stuff: it was in such short supply in 2016 that one UK supermarket withdrew Prosecco bottles from its shelves. With freakish hot and cold weather becoming the norm, there's concern over future supplies, too.

# Harry's Concoction

The world's first bellini was actually made with Prosecco, not Champagne – it was invented in 1948 in Venice's famous Harry's Bar.

**"**

*Too much of anything is bad. But too much Champagne is just right.***"**

**"**

**F. Scott Fitzgerald**

*Fitzgerald used to be a regular at Harry's Bar, so perhaps he said the same about Prosecco, too.*

# Vine Thieves

Making Prosecco is big business, so much so that there's a black market and thieves are visiting vineyards in Italy's Veneto and Friuli-Venezia-Giulia regions late at night to steal freshly planted vines. The owners are fighting back: one tactic is to spray the plants with a coloured dye.

# Prosecco Imitators

European regulators have been able to force a name change for Croatian "Prosek" in 2013 (and it wasn't even a similar-style wine), but they have no jurisdiction outside of Europe – hence Espumante Garibaldi Prosecco from Brazil and Vintage Pucino Prosecco from Australia finding their way to wine racks.

# Australian "Prosecco Road"

There's a Prosecco Road in the King Valley River wine-producing region in Victoria, Australia. Inspired by his birthplace in Italy's Valdobbiadene, Otto Dal Zotto was the first to plant cuttings taken from vines in Italy in the 1990s, and now there are five producers in the region.

**"**

*I may not speak Italian but I'm fluent in Prosecco!*

**"**

**Unknown**

# Most Impressive Prosecco Festival

You'll need to travel to Italy to attend Vino in Villa, a Prosecco festival held at a castle in Italy's Prosecco region. Here you can sample Italy's best Prosecco – Conegliano Valdobbiadene Prosecco Superiore DOCG – and wander around the grounds of the medieval San Salvatore Castle, which even has a drawbridge.

# Day Trip from Venice

The Italian wine-growing region that produces Prosecco is only an hour away from Venice, making it the perfect day-trip destination if you happen to be staying in the "City of Canals". What better way to try Prosecco that to enjoy a wine-tasting experience at a vincyard, or two, or...?

# From Sauvignon Blanc to Prosecco

Graham Norton is often seen with a glass of white wine when hosting his late-night chat show, but perhaps not many people know the TV presenter has also produced a top-selling Sauvignon Blanc. Or that his latest adventure is his very own sparkling wine, called Graham Norton's Own Prosecco.

# Supermodel Collection

She may be better known for her marriage to Billy Joel and her modelling career, but Christie Brinkley has also launched her own brand of Prosecco, called Bellissima (Italian for "most beautiful"). Perhaps unsurprisingly with a model at the helm, the wine label includes a zero sugar version.

# Prosecco Smile

Regardless of what F. Scott Fitzgerald might think (see page 109), you can have too much Prosecco – the Italian bubbly can lead to "Prosecco smile" over time. The combination of carbonation, sweetness and alcohol can result in enamel erosion.

**"**

*Start the day
with a smile, end it
with Prosecco.*

**"**

Unknown

# Why is Prosecco Considered a Wine?

A wine is an alcoholic drink made from fermented grape juice, which is exactly how Prosecco is produced, so technically Prosecco is a wine. Because it is made with only white grapes, it falls into the white wine category.

**"**

*Throw confetti, pop some Prosecco and toast to a new year.*

**"**

Unknown

# Prosecco Vending Machine

The premium Prosecco Superiore di Cartizze hails from Collina del Cartizze. This hill is also where you can find a Prosecco vending machine, on La Strada del Prosecco (Prosecco Road).

If you can't find it on a map, look for Osteria Senz'Oste, the farmhouse restaurant and landmark.

# The Host-free Osteria

Osteria Senz'Oste is Italian for "tavern without a host", and if you come across it when looking for the vending machine on Prosecco Road (it's impossible to miss), it's worth stopping to enjoy the cheese, salami and other local meats. It runs on the honour system – don't forget to pay before you leave.

# Automated Prosecco Machine

In January 2020, to promote the opening of a new bar in an old bank, free Prosecco was dispensed from a spout installed in an ATM, or APM (automated Prosecco machine). But Italian winemakers weren't happy about the free-flowing Prosecco. According to EU regulations, Prosecco must be served from a bottle.

# Prosecco on Tap

Some British pubs have served "Prosecco" on tap. But the Prosecco Consortium has pointed out that not only is it illegal, the carbon dioxide used in tap systems will ruin the taste – and they're worried about Prosecco's reputation. They want the tap wine to be called by another name. Any suggestions?

# Such a Waste

In 2017, experts warned that about 40 per cent of us used "incorrect pouring methods" that led to wasting Prosecco by overflowing glasses, mostly when removing the cork.

And it gets worse: one in four 18–24 year-olds admit to spilling the bubbly while dancing.

# Exploding Tank

The day a fermentation tank was overfilled and exploded, the loss of 30,000 litres (8,000 gallons) of Prosecco was captured on film and went viral on social media, with more than one million views on Facebook. Prosecco lovers from around the world offered to travel to Italy to help – and bring some glasses or straws.

# Shattering Bottles

In 2015, thousands of bottles of one brand of Prosecco had to be recalled: they were randomly shattering and exploding.

As there was a concern about an impeding worldwide shortage of Prosecco at the time, one wine society warned its members to stock up "on the safe stuff now".

# No to Nosecco

A French company launched an alcohol-free sparkling wine named "Nosecco" in 2017. That was a no-no. When taken to court, the French company lost by referring to Nosecco as a "parody of Prosecco" and its "witty nature" in the evidence; the court ruled they instead "made the case" that Nosecco evoked Prosecco.

# Prosecco & Pink Peppercorn Crisps

The Italian government confiscated 250 tubes of Prosecco and pink peppercorn-flavoured crisps, intended for the UK market but sold in a supermarket in Italy's Veneto region. The company was accused of identity theft, but it says it followed DOC guidelines and EU regulations.

They have no plans to "produce this variant in the future".

**“**

*Yet another scam by a British company to the detriment of Prosecco PDO in the United Kingdom, after the sale of fake Prosecco on tap in pubs, and Prosecco-flavoured sweets, crisps and tea bags in supermarkets.*

**”**

Excerpt of the formal complaint entered by an Italian Member of the European Parliament (MEP) to the European Commission.

CHAPTER
**FIVE**

# Cocktails & Punches

The classics, with a splash
of modern twists.

**"**

*It's beginning
to look a lot
like cocktails.*

**"**

**Unknown**

# Sgroppino

This recipe dates back to fifteenth-century Venice, when it was used as a refreshing palate cleanser between courses at an aristocratic dinner party.

*30ml (1fl oz) vodka, chilled*
*Scoop of lemon sorbet*
*Prosecco, chilled*

Put all three well-chilled ingredients into a blender and blitz. Serve in a cold glass.

# Aperol Spritz

*3 parts Aperol\**
*2 parts Prosecco*
*Dash of soda water*
*Orange Slice*
*Ice*

Combine the Prosecco with the Aperol in an ice-filled glass, then top with the soda water and garnish with the slice of orange.

*\*This classic Italian bitter liqueur is made from a herbal infusion that includes orange and rhubarb.*

# Grapefruit Aperol Spritz

*2 parts grapefruit juice*
*1 part Aperol*
*2 parts Prosecco*
*Twist of grapefruit zest (optional)*

Pour the grapefruit juice and Aperol
into a chilled glass, add
ice and stir. Top up with
Prosecco and garnish with a
grapefruit twist, if using.

# Prosecco Royale

*2–3 teaspoons crème de cassis\**
*3–4 raspberries (optional)*
*Prosecco*

Add the crème de cassis to the
glass and top with the raspberries,
if using, then fill the glass with
Prosecco.

*\*You can substitute the crème de cassis with
crème de framboise or Chambord.*

# Slow Royale

*25ml (¾fl oz) sloe gin*
*Prosecco*
*Edible glitter (optional)*

Pour the gin into a glass and
top up with Prosecco. Sprinkle the
edible glitter on top before serving,
if you wish.

**66**

*Sunday is for poppin' bottles.*

**99**

**Unknown**

# Mimosa

*1 part Prosecco*
*1 part freshly squeezed*
*orange juice*

Pour the Prosecco into the glass,
add the orange juice and sip.
For a fancy twist, add a splash
of pineapple, pomegranate or
cranberry juice, or add a little
chopped-up fresh strawberries
or orange pieces to the bottom
of the glass.

# Bellini

*1 part peach purée\**
*2 parts Prosecco*

First add the peach purée to your glass, then top up with Prosecco.

*\*To make your own peach purée, process a few peeled white or yellow peach wedges with 2 teaspoons of sugar in a food processor.*

# Bellini Variations

Substitute the peach purée
with peach nectar.

Try a different flavour by substituting
the peach purée for a raspberry purée.

Make a frozen bellini by using
a frozen fruit purée.

# Rossini

A strawberry version of the bellini, named for the famous Italian composer.

*1 part strawberry purée\**
*3 parts Prosecco*

Add the strawberry purée to a glass, then top up with the Prosecco.

*\*To make your own strawberry purée, blend 3 ripe strawberries, hulled, with 1 teaspoon of sugar and a squeeze of lemon juice in a blender.*

# Hibiscus Prosecco

*Hibiscus flower (from a bottle)\**
*1 tablespoon hibiscus syrup (from
the hibiscus flower bottle)*
*Prosecco*

Place the flower and syrup in
the bottom of the glass, then
fill with Prosecco.

*\*Look for hibiscus flowers in syrup from a cook's
specialist shop – the flower can be eaten and has raspberry
and rhubarb flavours.*

# The Hugo

For a light summery drink.

*Mint leaves*
*Lime wedge*
*1–2 teaspoons elderflower cordial*
*20ml (¾fl oz) soda water*
*Prosecco*

Add plenty of ice, the mint leaves and lime wedge to a glass, then add the elderflower cordial and soda water and stir to combine. Top up with Prosecco and serve.

# Elderflower Gin Fizz

If you prefer a drink that has more of a kick, try this gin-based cocktail.

*50ml (1½fl oz) gin*
*30ml (1fl oz) elderflower cordial*
*15ml (½fl oz) lemon juice*
*Prosecco*
*Citrus slices and mint leaves*

Mix the gin and cordial in a shaker filled with ice, strain into a glass and top up with Prosecco before garnishing with the citrus and mint.

# Rose-ecco

Sophie Dahl is credited with this rosy cocktail.

*Prosecco*
*1½–2 tablespoons rose syrup*
*A few raspberries or other berries*
*(optional)*

Fill a glass with Prosecco, then drizzle in the syrup and allow it to trickle to the bottom of the glass. Add ice and garnish with a few raspberries, if you wish.

# Lavender Prosecco

*1 tablespoon lavender syrup*
*1 teaspoon lemon juice*
*Prosecco*
*Fresh lavender flowers and*
*lemon slice (optional)*

Add the lavender syrup and lemon
juice to a glass, then fill with Prosecco.
Garnish with lavender and a lemon
slice, if you wish.

# Bakewell Fizz

Perfect for sipping in front a fire on a cold winter day. For a festive treat, try sprinkling ¼ teaspoon of edible rose gold glitter on top.

*Kirsch-soaked cherry*
*1 tablespoon kirsch*
*1 part amaretto*
*3 parts Prosecco*

Add the cherry to the bottom of the glass, then add the kirsch, amaretto and Prosecco.

# Cherry and Citrus Spritz

*2 parts cherry liqueur*
*1 part gin*
*1 part lemon juice*
*1 part orange juice*
*Prosecco*
*Candied cherries and orange slice*

Stir the cherry liqueur, gin, lemon juice
and orange juice in a cocktail shaker.
Strain into ice-filled glasses and top with
Prosecco. Garnish with a few cherries
and an orange slice.

# Prosecco Margarita

*Lime slices*
*Coarse salt*
*50ml (1½fl oz) white tequila*
*60ml (2fl oz) lime juice*
*20ml (¾fl oz) Triple Sec or Cointreau*
*Dash of agave syrup*
*Prosecco*

Prepare the glasses first: rub a slice of lime around the rim of the glass, then dip it in a shallow dish of the salt.

Combine the tequila, lime juice, Triple Sec or Cointreau and the syrup, pour carefully into the glass to avoid disturbing the salt, and top up with Prosecco.

For serving at a party, you can make this in bulk, minus the Prosecco - add it at the last minute to maintain the bubbles.

# Pink Gin Fizz

The difficult part might be deciding which pink gin to choose. Check the label – different fruits are used to obtain the pink colour, and some even include pink peppercorns.

*50ml (1½fl oz) pink gin*
*50ml (1½fl oz) lemonade*
*Prosecco*

After combining the gin and lemonade in a glass, top up with Prosecco.

# Negroni Sbagliato

When a bartender in Milan added sparkling wine to a negroni in 1972, he mistakenly invented this cocktail (*sbagliato* is Italian for "mistaken").

*1 part sweet vermouth*
*1 part Campari*
*1 part Prosecco*
*Orange slice*

Mix together the three ingredients with ice in a glass and garnish with an orange slice.

# Porn Star Martini

You can thank Douglas Ankrah
for inventing this cocktail in a London
bar in 2002.

*3 parts vanilla-flavoured vodka*
*1 part passionfruit liqueur*
*2 parts passionfruit purée*
*1 part lime juice*
*1 part vanilla simple syrup*
*Passionfruit slice*
*4 parts Prosecco, chilled*

Add the vodka, fruit liqueur, fruit purée, lime juice and simple syrup to a cocktail shaker with ice, then shake vigorously. It should be well-chilled.

Strain into a chilled coupe glass and garnish with the passionfruit slice. Serve with a chilled shot glass of Prosecco on the side*.

*Either sip the Prosecco, alternating with the cocktail as per the original recipe, or pour it over the cocktail before drinking it.*

# Pear Prosecco

*1 tablespoon sugar*
*½ teaspoon ground cinnamon*
*1 tablespoon ginger syrup (from
a jar of preserved ginger)*
*1 part pear juice*
*1 part Prosecco*

Mix the sugar and cinnamon in a
dish. Dip the rim of the glass in the
water, then the cinnamon mix.
Pour the ginger syrup into the
glass, then top with the pear juice
and Prosecco.

# Apple Cider Prosecco

*1 tablespoon sugar*
*½ teaspoon ground cinnamon*
*1 part brandy*
*2 parts apple cider*
*Prosecco*

Mix the sugar and cinnamon
in a shallow dish. Dip the rim of the
glass into some apple cider, then
into the cinnamon mix. Pour the
brandy and apple cider into the
glass, then top with the Prosecco.

# Christmas Prosecco Punch

Most of the preparation can be done in advance, making this punch perfect for serving at a party or large gathering.

*2 litres (3½ pints/8½ cups)
cranberry juice
700ml (1¼ pints/3 cups)
pomegranate juice
500ml (17fl oz/2 cups) clementine
or orange juice
Juice of 2 limes*

*3 limes, sliced*
*3 clementines, sliced*
*100g (3½oz/1 cup) fresh*
*or frozen cranberries*
*Seeds from 1 pomegranate*
*1 bottle Prosecco*
*300ml (10fl oz/1¼ cups) vodka*
*Small bunch of fresh mint leaves*

Mix together all the juices and prepared fruit in a punch bowl or jug, and refrigerate for up to 3 hours. When ready to serve, stir in the Prosecco and vodka, add ice and scatter with mint leaves.

# Apple Prosecco Punch

*400ml (14fl oz/1¾ cups) cloudy
apple juice
200ml (7fl oz/¾ cup) vodka
Juice of 2 lemons
1 bottle Prosecco
1 apple, cored and finely sliced*

Pour the apple juice, vodka and lemon
juice into a punch bowl or large jug,
stir and chill for up to 2 hours.
When ready to serve, add the Prosecco,
apple slices and ice.

# Blood Orange Mule

*Juice of ½ a blood orange, plus a slice*
*Juice of ½ a lime*
*30ml (1fl oz) vodka*
*60ml (2fl oz) ginger beer, chilled*
*Prosecco*
*Mint leaves*

Combine the orange juice, lime
juice and vodka in a glass. Add the
ginger beer and top up with Prosecco.
Add a blood orange slice and garnish
with mint leaves.

CHAPTER
**SIX**

# Popping Out

Bubbly quotes and proverbs.

**"**

*Let's celebrate everything with a little bit of Prosecco.*

**"**

**Unknown**

**"**

*All you need is love, laughter and Prosecco.*

**"**

**Unknown**

**66**

*Meet my best friend – she's my partner in Prosecco.*

**99**

**Unknown**

**66**

*Amici e vini sono meglio vecchi – Friends and wine improve with age.*

**99**

**Italian proverb**

*Italians place a lot of value on both friendship and their love of wine. This proverb sums up how they both improve with the passing of time.*

**"**

*A San Martino ogni mosto diventa vino – When St Martin's day arrives, the must turns into wine.*

**"**

**Italian proverb**

*St Martin's day is in November, around the time new wine from recently harvest grapes is ready to drink, so the proverb means, whether we're ready for it or not, the time for change will always arrive.*

**66**

*I'll be ready in
a Prosecco.*

**99**

Unknown

**66**

*Nel vino c'è la verità – In wine there is truth.*

**99**

**Latin proverb**

*The same as the Italian* in vino veritas, *a reminder that inebriation can lower inhibitions and loosen lips – it's so old that even Pliny the Elder (first century AD) is known to have mentioned it.*

**"**

*The wine cup is the little silver well, where truth, if truth there be, doth dwell.*

**"**

**William Shakespeare (1564–1616)**

**"**

# *A man will be eloquent if you give him good wine.*

**"**

**Ralph Waldo Emerson (1803–1882)**

> **"**
>
> *Dire pane al pane e vino al vino – Call bread bread and wine wine.*
>
> **"**

**Italian proverb**

*You should speak honestly and plainly about something by calling it by its right name.*

**66**

*Quickly, bring me a beaker of wine, so that I may wet my mind and say something clever.*

**99**

**Aristophanes (450–385 BC)**

**66**

*In a Prosecco
state of mind.*

**99**

**Unknown**

**"**

*Let us have wine and women, mirth and laughter,*

*Sermons and soda water the day after.*

**"**

**Lord Byron (1788–1824)**

**"**

*When there is plenty of wine, sorry and worry take wing.*

**"**

Ovid (43 BC–AD 17)

**"**

*Chi non beve in compagnia o è un ladro o è una spia –*
*People who do not drink with others are either thieves or spies.*

**"**

**Italian proverb**

*There must be a reason why someone is not willing to have a drink when invited, such as being wary of accidentally telling a secret.*

**180**

66

*Prosecco is always
the answer.*

99

**Unknown**

66

*There are so many beautiful reasons to be happy. Prosecco is one of them.*

99

**Unknown**

**66**

*No use crying over spilled Prosecco.*

**99**

Julie James, greatsayings.net

**"**

*True friends don't walk out the door when things get tough. They pour Prosecco and pull up a chair.*

**"**

Unknown

66

*Wishing you peace, love and lots of Prosecco in the new year.*

99

Unknown

**"**

*Prosecco is informal, spontaneous and free from rituals.*

**"**

**Chloe Delevingne,** *Cosmopolitan*

**66**

*I'm here because
I was told there
would be Prosecco.*

**99**

**Unknown**

**66**

*That Prosecco don't got you feelin' like Rihanna.*

**99**

**Jacob Banks, in his song "Prosecco"**

66

*I like my wine
sparkling, like
my personality.*

99

**Unknown**

**66**

*Good wine is a necessity of life for me.*

**99**

**Thomas Jefferson (1743–1826)**

**66**

*No thing more excellent nor more valuable than wine was ever granted mankind by God.*

**99**

**Plato (400 BC)**

**"**

*Drink wine, and you will sleep well. Sleep well, and you will not sin. Avoid sin, and you will be saved. Ergo, drink wine and be saved.*

**"**

**Medieval German proverb**